50 Old Quebec Recipes

By: Kelly Johnson

Table of Contents

- Tourtière (Meat Pie)
- Poutine à la Viande (Meat Poutine)
- Cretons (Pork Spread)
- Cipaille (Layered Meat Pie)
- Soupe aux Pois (Pea Soup)
- Pouding Chômeur (Poor Man's Pudding)
- Tarte au Sucre (Sugar Pie)
- Fèves au Lard (Baked Beans)
- Ragoût de Pattes de Cochon (Pork Hock Stew)
- Oreilles de Crisse (Crispy Pork Rinds)
- Pâté Chinois (Shepherd's Pie)
- Grand-Pères au Sirop d'Érable (Dumplings in Maple Syrup)
- Pain de Ménage (Homemade Bread)
- Tarte aux Bleuets (Blueberry Pie)
- Bouilli Québécois (Boiled Dinner)
- Salade de Choux Crémeuse (Creamy Coleslaw)
- Ragoût de Boulettes (Meatball Stew)
- Pets de Sœur (Cinnamon Rolls)
- Poulet à la Québécoise (Quebec-Style Chicken)
- Beignes à l'Ancienne (Old-Fashioned Doughnuts)
- Tarte aux Pommes Québécoise (Quebec Apple Pie)
- Gourgane Soup (Fava Bean Soup)
- Pouding aux Pommes (Apple Pudding)
- Soupe à l'Oignon Gratinée (French Onion Soup)
- Pommes de Terre Farcies (Stuffed Potatoes)
- Cipâte à la Mode du Lac-Saint-Jean (Traditional Meat Pie)
- Beurre de Pommes (Apple Butter)
- Chômeur aux Petits Fruits (Berry Pouding Chômeur)
- Gâteau Reine Élizabeth (Queen Elizabeth Cake)
- Sauce Brune Maison (Homemade Brown Gravy)
- Lapin à la Moutarde (Rabbit in Mustard Sauce)
- Flanc aux Oeufs (Egg Flan)
- Pouding au Pain à l'Érable (Maple Bread Pudding)
- Pâté au Saumon (Salmon Pie)
- Pommes de Terre au Gratin Québécois (Quebec Scalloped Potatoes)

- Croustade aux Pommes et à l'Érable (Apple Maple Crisp)
- Fromage en Grains Frit (Fried Cheese Curds)
- Riz au Lait à l'Érable (Maple Rice Pudding)
- Poulet Rôti aux Herbes (Herb-Roasted Chicken)
- Pain de Viande Québécois (Quebec Meatloaf)
- Confiture de Petits Fruits (Mixed Berry Jam)
- Ragoût de Gibier (Game Meat Stew)
- Poires Pochées au Sirop d'Érable (Maple Poached Pears)
- Truite Fumée au Bois d'Érable (Maple-Smoked Trout)
- Salade de Betteraves et Fromage de Chèvre (Beet and Goat Cheese Salad)
- Soufflé au Sirop d'Érable (Maple Syrup Soufflé)
- Cassoulet Québécois (Quebec-Style Cassoulet)
- Gâteau aux Fruits à l'Ancienne (Old-Fashioned Fruit Cake)
- Oeufs en Gelée (Eggs in Aspic)
- Pain d'Épices Québécois (Quebec Gingerbread)

Tourtière (Meat Pie)

Ingredients

- 1 lb ground pork (or a mix of pork and beef)
- 1/2 cup onion, finely chopped
- 1/2 tsp salt
- 1/2 tsp black pepper
- 1/2 tsp cinnamon
- 1/4 tsp cloves
- 1/2 cup beef or chicken broth
- 1 double pie crust

Instructions

1. Preheat oven to 375°F (190°C).
2. In a pan, cook pork and onion until browned.
3. Add salt, pepper, cinnamon, cloves, and broth. Simmer until liquid reduces.
4. Fill the pie crust, cover with the second crust, and seal edges.
5. Bake for 40-45 minutes until golden brown.

Poutine à la Viande (Meat Poutine)

Ingredients

- 4 cups French fries, cooked
- 1 cup shredded beef or pork
- 1 cup beef gravy
- 1/2 cup cheese curds

Instructions

1. Layer fries on a plate and top with shredded meat.
2. Sprinkle cheese curds over the meat.
3. Pour hot beef gravy on top and serve immediately.

Cretons (Pork Spread)

Ingredients

- 1 lb ground pork
- 1/2 cup milk
- 1/2 cup breadcrumbs
- 1 small onion, minced
- 1/2 tsp salt
- 1/2 tsp black pepper
- 1/2 tsp cinnamon
- 1/4 tsp cloves

Instructions

1. In a saucepan, combine all ingredients.
2. Cook on low heat for 1 hour, stirring occasionally.
3. Blend until smooth, then cool before refrigerating.
4. Serve on toast or crackers.

Cipaille (Layered Meat Pie)

Ingredients

- 1 lb cubed pork
- 1 lb cubed beef
- 1 lb cubed chicken
- 1/2 cup onion, chopped
- 1/2 tsp salt
- 1/2 tsp pepper
- 1/2 tsp thyme
- 2 cups beef or chicken broth
- 1 double pie crust

Instructions

1. Preheat oven to 350°F (175°C).
2. In a baking dish, layer meats and onions, seasoning each layer.
3. Pour in broth and cover with a pie crust.
4. Bake for 3-4 hours until tender.

Soupe aux Pois (Pea Soup)

Ingredients

- 2 cups dried yellow split peas
- 1/2 lb salt pork, diced
- 1 onion, chopped
- 2 carrots, diced
- 6 cups water
- 1/2 tsp thyme
- Salt and pepper to taste

Instructions

1. Rinse peas and soak overnight.
2. In a pot, sauté salt pork and onion until softened.
3. Add peas, carrots, water, and thyme.
4. Simmer for 1.5-2 hours until thick.

Pouding Chômeur (Poor Man's Pudding)

Ingredients

- 1 cup flour
- 1 tsp baking powder
- 1/4 tsp salt
- 1/2 cup sugar
- 1/2 cup milk
- 1/4 cup butter, melted
- 1 cup maple syrup
- 1 cup hot water

Instructions

1. Preheat oven to 350°F (175°C). Grease a baking dish.
2. In a bowl, mix flour, baking powder, salt, sugar, milk, and butter. Pour batter into the dish.
3. In a saucepan, heat maple syrup and hot water. Pour over batter.
4. Bake for 35 minutes until golden.

Tarte au Sucre (Sugar Pie)

Ingredients

- 1 pie crust
- 1 cup brown sugar
- 1/2 cup heavy cream
- 1/4 cup butter, melted
- 1 tbsp flour
- 1/2 tsp vanilla extract

Instructions

1. Preheat oven to 350°F (175°C).
2. In a bowl, mix brown sugar, cream, butter, flour, and vanilla.
3. Pour into pie crust and bake for 35 minutes.

Fèves au Lard (Baked Beans)

Ingredients

- 2 cups dried navy beans
- 1/2 cup maple syrup
- 1/4 cup molasses
- 1 small onion, chopped
- 1/2 cup salt pork, diced
- 1/2 tsp mustard
- 4 cups water

Instructions

1. Soak beans overnight, then drain.
2. Preheat oven to 300°F (150°C).
3. In a baking dish, mix beans, syrup, molasses, onion, salt pork, mustard, and water.
4. Cover and bake for 4-5 hours, stirring occasionally.

Ragoût de Pattes de Cochon (Pork Hock Stew)

Ingredients

- 2 pork hocks, cleaned
- 1/2 cup flour
- 4 cups water
- 1 onion, chopped
- 2 cloves garlic, minced
- 1/2 tsp cinnamon
- 1/2 tsp cloves
- Salt and pepper to taste

Instructions

1. Dredge pork hocks in flour and brown in a pot.
2. Add water, onion, garlic, cinnamon, cloves, salt, and pepper.
3. Simmer for 2 hours until tender.

Oreilles de Crisse (Crispy Pork Rinds)

Ingredients

- 1 lb salt pork, sliced thin
- Vegetable oil for frying

Instructions

1. Heat oil to 350°F (175°C).
2. Fry salt pork in batches until crispy and golden.
3. Drain on paper towels and serve hot.

Pâté Chinois (Shepherd's Pie)

Ingredients

- 1 lb ground beef
- 1 onion, chopped
- 3 cups mashed potatoes
- 2 cups canned corn
- Salt and pepper to taste

Instructions

1. Preheat oven to 375°F (190°C).
2. Brown beef and onion in a skillet, seasoning with salt and pepper.
3. Layer meat, corn, and mashed potatoes in a baking dish.
4. Bake for 30 minutes until golden on top.

Grand-Pères au Sirop d'Érable (Dumplings in Maple Syrup)

Ingredients

- 1 cup flour
- 1 tsp baking powder
- 1/4 tsp salt
- 2 tbsp butter, softened
- 1/3 cup milk
- 2 cups maple syrup
- 1 cup water

Instructions

1. In a saucepan, bring maple syrup and water to a boil.
2. In a bowl, mix flour, baking powder, salt, butter, and milk into a soft dough.
3. Drop spoonfuls of dough into syrup and simmer for 10 minutes.

Pain de Ménage (Homemade Bread)

Ingredients

- 4 cups flour
- 2 tsp salt
- 2 tbsp sugar
- 1 tbsp yeast
- 1 1/2 cups warm water

Instructions

1. Dissolve yeast in warm water with sugar and let sit for 5 minutes.
2. Mix flour and salt, then stir in yeast mixture. Knead for 10 minutes.
3. Let rise for 1 hour, then shape into a loaf.
4. Bake at 375°F (190°C) for 30 minutes.

Tarte aux Bleuets (Blueberry Pie)

Ingredients

- 1 pie crust
- 3 cups blueberries
- 3/4 cup sugar
- 2 tbsp cornstarch
- 1 tbsp lemon juice

Instructions

1. Preheat oven to 375°F (190°C).
2. Mix blueberries, sugar, cornstarch, and lemon juice. Pour into crust.
3. Bake for 40 minutes until bubbly.

Bouilli Québécois (Boiled Dinner)

Ingredients

- 1 lb beef brisket
- 4 potatoes, peeled and chopped
- 3 carrots, sliced
- 1 turnip, diced
- 1 small cabbage, quartered
- 6 cups water
- 1/2 tsp salt
- 1/2 tsp pepper

Instructions

1. Bring water to a boil and add beef, salt, and pepper. Simmer for 1 hour.
2. Add vegetables and cook until tender.

Salade de Choux Crémeuse (Creamy Coleslaw)

Ingredients

- 4 cups cabbage, shredded
- 1/2 cup carrots, grated
- 1/2 cup mayonnaise
- 1 tbsp apple cider vinegar
- 1 tbsp sugar
- 1/2 tsp salt

Instructions

1. Mix cabbage and carrots in a bowl.
2. In another bowl, whisk mayonnaise, vinegar, sugar, and salt.
3. Toss with cabbage mixture and chill before serving.

Ragoût de Boulettes (Meatball Stew)

Ingredients

- 1 lb ground pork
- 1/2 cup breadcrumbs
- 1 egg
- 1/2 tsp cinnamon
- 1/2 tsp salt
- 1/4 tsp cloves
- 3 cups beef broth

Instructions

1. Mix pork, breadcrumbs, egg, cinnamon, salt, and cloves. Shape into meatballs.
2. Brown meatballs in a skillet, then transfer to a pot with broth.
3. Simmer for 30 minutes.

Pets de Sœur (Cinnamon Rolls)

Ingredients

- 1 pie crust
- 1/4 cup brown sugar
- 2 tbsp butter, melted
- 1 tsp cinnamon

Instructions

1. Preheat oven to 375°F (190°C).
2. Roll out pie crust and brush with melted butter.
3. Sprinkle with brown sugar and cinnamon. Roll up and slice into pieces.
4. Bake for 15 minutes.

Poulet à la Québécoise (Quebec-Style Chicken)

Ingredients

- 1 whole chicken, cut into pieces
- 1 onion, chopped
- 1/2 cup maple syrup
- 1/4 cup Dijon mustard
- 1/2 tsp thyme
- Salt and pepper to taste

Instructions

1. Preheat oven to 375°F (190°C).
2. Mix maple syrup, mustard, thyme, salt, and pepper.
3. Place chicken in a baking dish, coat with mixture, and bake for 45 minutes.

Beignes à l'Ancienne (Old-Fashioned Doughnuts)

Ingredients

- 3 cups all-purpose flour
- 2 tsp baking powder
- 1/2 tsp salt
- 1/2 tsp nutmeg
- 1/2 cup sugar
- 2 eggs
- 1/2 cup milk
- 1/4 cup butter, melted
- 1 tsp vanilla extract
- Oil for frying

Instructions

1. In a bowl, mix flour, baking powder, salt, and nutmeg.
2. In another bowl, whisk sugar, eggs, milk, butter, and vanilla.
3. Combine wet and dry ingredients, knead lightly, and roll out dough.
4. Cut into doughnut shapes and fry in hot oil at 350°F (175°C) until golden.
5. Drain on paper towels and dust with sugar.

Tarte aux Pommes Québécoise (Quebec Apple Pie)

Ingredients

- 1 pie crust
- 4 apples, peeled and sliced
- 1/2 cup brown sugar
- 1 tsp cinnamon
- 1 tbsp flour
- 1 tbsp butter, diced

Instructions

1. Preheat oven to 375°F (190°C).
2. Toss apples with sugar, cinnamon, and flour.
3. Arrange apples in the pie crust, dot with butter, and bake for 40-45 minutes.

Gourgane Soup (Fava Bean Soup)

Ingredients

- 2 cups dried fava beans, soaked overnight
- 1 small onion, chopped
- 2 carrots, diced
- 1 potato, diced
- 4 cups vegetable broth
- 1/2 tsp thyme
- Salt and pepper to taste

Instructions

1. Drain soaked fava beans and rinse.
2. In a pot, sauté onion until soft. Add beans, carrots, potatoes, broth, and thyme.
3. Simmer for 1 hour, stirring occasionally.

Pouding aux Pommes (Apple Pudding)

Ingredients

- 3 apples, peeled and diced
- 1 cup flour
- 1/2 cup sugar
- 1 tsp baking powder
- 1/2 cup milk
- 1/4 cup butter, melted
- 1 tsp cinnamon

Instructions

1. Preheat oven to 350°F (175°C). Grease a baking dish.
2. Mix flour, sugar, and baking powder.
3. Stir in milk, butter, and apples, then pour into the dish.
4. Sprinkle with cinnamon and bake for 35 minutes.

Soupe à l'Oignon Gratinée (French Onion Soup)

Ingredients

- 4 onions, thinly sliced
- 2 tbsp butter
- 4 cups beef broth
- 1/2 cup white wine
- 1/2 tsp thyme
- Salt and pepper to taste
- 4 slices baguette
- 1 cup grated Gruyère cheese

Instructions

1. Sauté onions in butter until caramelized.
2. Add broth, wine, thyme, salt, and pepper. Simmer for 30 minutes.
3. Ladle soup into bowls, top with baguette slices and cheese, then broil until golden.

Pommes de Terre Farcies (Stuffed Potatoes)

Ingredients

- 4 large potatoes, baked
- 1/2 cup cheddar cheese, shredded
- 1/4 cup sour cream
- 1/4 cup cooked bacon, crumbled
- 2 tbsp chives, chopped
- Salt and pepper to taste

Instructions

1. Cut baked potatoes in half and scoop out flesh into a bowl.
2. Mix with cheese, sour cream, bacon, chives, salt, and pepper.
3. Refill potato skins and bake at 375°F (190°C) for 15 minutes.

Cipâte à la Mode du Lac-Saint-Jean (Traditional Meat Pie)

Ingredients

- 1 lb cubed pork
- 1 lb cubed beef
- 1 lb cubed chicken
- 2 potatoes, diced
- 1 onion, chopped
- 1/2 tsp thyme
- Salt and pepper to taste
- 2 cups beef broth
- 1 double pie crust

Instructions

1. Preheat oven to 325°F (160°C).
2. In a baking dish, layer meats, potatoes, and onion, seasoning each layer.
3. Pour in broth and cover with pie crust.
4. Bake for 4-5 hours until tender.

Beurre de Pommes (Apple Butter)

Ingredients

- 6 apples, peeled and chopped
- 1/2 cup brown sugar
- 1/2 tsp cinnamon
- 1/4 tsp nutmeg
- 1 tsp vanilla extract
- 1/2 cup water

Instructions

1. In a slow cooker, combine apples, sugar, cinnamon, nutmeg, vanilla, and water.
2. Cook on low for 6-8 hours, stirring occasionally.
3. Blend until smooth and store in jars.

Chômeur aux Petits Fruits (Berry Pouding Chômeur)

Ingredients

- 1 cup mixed berries (blueberries, raspberries)
- 1 cup flour
- 1 tsp baking powder
- 1/2 cup sugar
- 1/2 cup milk
- 1/4 cup butter, melted
- 1 cup maple syrup

Instructions

1. Preheat oven to 350°F (175°C). Grease a baking dish.
2. Mix flour, baking powder, sugar, milk, and butter.
3. Spread berries in the dish and pour batter over them.
4. Heat maple syrup and pour over batter.
5. Bake for 35 minutes until golden.

Gâteau Reine Élizabeth (Queen Elizabeth Cake)

Ingredients

- 1 cup dates, chopped
- 1 cup boiling water
- 1 tsp baking soda
- 1 cup sugar
- 1/4 cup butter
- 1 egg
- 1 1/2 cups flour
- 1 tsp baking powder
- 1/2 tsp salt
- 1/2 tsp vanilla

Topping

- 1/2 cup brown sugar
- 1/4 cup butter
- 1/4 cup milk
- 1/2 cup shredded coconut

Instructions

1. Preheat oven to 350°F (175°C). Grease a cake pan.
2. Pour boiling water over dates and baking soda. Let cool.
3. In a bowl, cream sugar and butter, then beat in egg and vanilla.
4. Add flour, baking powder, and salt, then fold in the date mixture.
5. Pour into the pan and bake for 35 minutes.
6. For topping, heat brown sugar, butter, and milk. Stir in coconut.
7. Spread over the cake and broil for 2 minutes until bubbly.

Sauce Brune Maison (Homemade Brown Gravy)

Ingredients

- 2 tbsp butter
- 2 tbsp flour
- 2 cups beef broth
- 1 tsp Worcestershire sauce
- Salt and pepper to taste

Instructions

1. In a saucepan, melt butter and whisk in flour. Cook for 2 minutes.
2. Gradually add beef broth, whisking constantly.
3. Stir in Worcestershire sauce, salt, and pepper. Simmer for 5 minutes.

Lapin à la Moutarde (Rabbit in Mustard Sauce)

Ingredients

- 1 rabbit, cut into pieces
- 1/4 cup Dijon mustard
- 1/2 cup white wine
- 1/2 cup chicken broth
- 1/2 cup heavy cream
- 2 tbsp butter
- 1 tbsp olive oil
- 1 tsp thyme
- Salt and pepper to taste

Instructions

1. Heat butter and oil in a pan. Brown rabbit pieces.
2. Spread mustard over the rabbit, then pour in wine and broth.
3. Cover and simmer for 45 minutes. Stir in cream and thyme.
4. Simmer for another 5 minutes before serving.

Flan aux Oeufs (Egg Flan)

Ingredients

- 2 cups milk
- 3 eggs
- 1/2 cup sugar
- 1 tsp vanilla extract
- 1/4 cup caramel sauce

Instructions

1. Preheat oven to 325°F (165°C).
2. Whisk eggs, sugar, vanilla, and milk together.
3. Pour caramel sauce into ramekins, then add egg mixture.
4. Place in a water bath and bake for 45 minutes.

Pouding au Pain à l'Érable (Maple Bread Pudding)

Ingredients

- 4 cups stale bread, cubed
- 2 cups milk
- 1/2 cup maple syrup
- 2 eggs
- 1 tsp cinnamon
- 1/2 tsp vanilla extract

Instructions

1. Preheat oven to 350°F (175°C).
2. Soak bread in milk for 10 minutes.
3. Whisk eggs, maple syrup, cinnamon, and vanilla, then mix with bread.
4. Pour into a baking dish and bake for 40 minutes.

Pâté au Saumon (Salmon Pie)

Ingredients

- 1 pie crust
- 2 cups cooked salmon, flaked
- 1/2 cup mashed potatoes
- 1/4 cup onion, chopped
- 1/2 tsp salt
- 1/4 tsp black pepper

Instructions

1. Preheat oven to 375°F (190°C).
2. Mix salmon, potatoes, onion, salt, and pepper.
3. Pour into the crust, top with another crust, and seal.
4. Bake for 40 minutes.

Pommes de Terre au Gratin Québécois (Quebec Scalloped Potatoes)

Ingredients

- 4 potatoes, thinly sliced
- 1 cup heavy cream
- 1 cup grated cheddar cheese
- 1/2 tsp salt
- 1/4 tsp black pepper

Instructions

1. Preheat oven to 375°F (190°C).
2. Layer potatoes in a baking dish, seasoning each layer.
3. Pour cream over potatoes and sprinkle with cheese.
4. Bake for 40 minutes.

Croustade aux Pommes et à l'Érable (Apple Maple Crisp)

Ingredients

- 4 apples, peeled and sliced
- 1/2 cup maple syrup
- 1/2 cup rolled oats
- 1/4 cup flour
- 1/4 cup butter, melted
- 1/2 tsp cinnamon

Instructions

1. Preheat oven to 375°F (190°C).
2. Toss apples with maple syrup and place in a baking dish.
3. Mix oats, flour, butter, and cinnamon.
4. Sprinkle over apples and bake for 30 minutes.

Fromage en Grains Frit (Fried Cheese Curds)

Ingredients

- 1 cup cheese curds
- 1/2 cup flour
- 1/2 cup breadcrumbs
- 1 egg
- Oil for frying

Instructions

1. Heat oil to 350°F (175°C).
2. Dip cheese curds in flour, then beaten egg, then breadcrumbs.
3. Fry until golden brown.

Riz au Lait à l'Érable (Maple Rice Pudding)

Ingredients

- 1/2 cup rice
- 2 cups milk
- 1/4 cup maple syrup
- 1/2 tsp cinnamon

Instructions

1. Simmer rice in milk until tender.
2. Stir in maple syrup and cinnamon.
3. Serve warm or chilled.

Poulet Rôti aux Herbes (Herb-Roasted Chicken)

Ingredients

- 1 whole chicken
- 2 tbsp butter, melted
- 1 tsp thyme
- 1 tsp rosemary
- 1/2 tsp salt
- 1/2 tsp black pepper

Instructions

1. Preheat oven to 375°F (190°C).
2. Rub chicken with butter and seasonings.
3. Roast for 1 hour, basting occasionally.

Pain de Viande Québécois (Quebec Meatloaf)

Ingredients

- 1 lb ground beef
- 1/2 cup breadcrumbs
- 1/4 cup ketchup
- 1 egg
- 1/2 tsp salt
- 1/4 tsp black pepper

Instructions

1. Preheat oven to 375°F (190°C).
2. Mix all ingredients and shape into a loaf.
3. Bake for 45 minutes.

Confiture de Petits Fruits (Mixed Berry Jam)

Ingredients

- 2 cups mixed berries (strawberries, raspberries, blueberries)
- 1 cup sugar
- 1 tbsp lemon juice
- 1 tsp pectin (optional)

Instructions

1. In a saucepan, mix berries, sugar, and lemon juice.
2. Simmer for 15-20 minutes, stirring frequently.
3. If using pectin, add in the last 5 minutes.
4. Let cool before storing in jars.

Ragoût de Gibier (Game Meat Stew)

Ingredients

- 1 lb game meat (venison, boar, or moose), cubed
- 1 onion, chopped
- 2 carrots, sliced
- 3 potatoes, diced
- 4 cups beef broth
- 1/2 cup red wine
- 2 tbsp flour
- 1/2 tsp thyme
- 1/2 tsp salt
- 1/4 tsp black pepper

Instructions

1. Brown game meat in a pot. Remove and set aside.
2. Sauté onion and carrots, then sprinkle with flour.
3. Add broth, wine, thyme, salt, and pepper. Return meat to the pot.
4. Simmer for 1.5 hours, adding potatoes in the last 30 minutes.

Poires Pochées au Sirop d'Érable (Maple Poached Pears)

Ingredients

- 4 pears, peeled and halved
- 2 cups water
- 1/2 cup maple syrup
- 1 cinnamon stick
- 1/2 tsp vanilla extract

Instructions

1. In a saucepan, bring water, maple syrup, cinnamon, and vanilla to a simmer.
2. Add pears and poach for 15-20 minutes until tender.
3. Serve warm with syrup drizzled over top.

Truite Fumée au Bois d'Érable (Maple-Smoked Trout)

Ingredients

- 2 trout fillets
- 1/4 cup maple syrup
- 1 tbsp salt
- 1/2 tsp black pepper
- Maple wood chips for smoking

Instructions

1. Rub trout with salt, pepper, and maple syrup. Let marinate for 1 hour.
2. Prepare smoker with maple wood chips.
3. Smoke trout at 200°F (95°C) for 1.5-2 hours.

Salade de Betteraves et Fromage de Chèvre (Beet and Goat Cheese Salad)

Ingredients

- 2 beets, roasted and sliced
- 4 cups mixed greens
- 1/4 cup goat cheese, crumbled
- 1/4 cup walnuts, toasted
- 2 tbsp balsamic vinegar
- 2 tbsp olive oil
- Salt and pepper to taste

Instructions

1. Toss greens with beets, goat cheese, and walnuts.
2. Drizzle with balsamic vinegar and olive oil.
3. Season with salt and pepper before serving.

Soufflé au Sirop d'Érable (Maple Syrup Soufflé)

Ingredients

- 3 eggs, separated
- 1/4 cup maple syrup
- 1 tbsp flour
- 1/2 cup milk
- 1/2 tsp vanilla extract

Instructions

1. Preheat oven to 375°F (190°C). Grease ramekins.
2. In a saucepan, heat maple syrup, flour, and milk, stirring until thickened.
3. Remove from heat, whisk in egg yolks and vanilla.
4. Beat egg whites until stiff, then fold into the mixture.
5. Pour into ramekins and bake for 15-18 minutes.

Cassoulet Québécois (Quebec-Style Cassoulet)

Ingredients

- 1 cup dried white beans, soaked overnight
- 1/2 lb duck confit or smoked pork
- 1/2 lb sausage, sliced
- 1 onion, chopped
- 2 cloves garlic, minced
- 1/2 tsp thyme
- 1/2 tsp black pepper
- 4 cups chicken broth

Instructions

1. In a pot, sauté onion and garlic. Add sausage and brown.
2. Stir in beans, duck confit, thyme, pepper, and broth.
3. Simmer for 1.5-2 hours until beans are tender.

Gâteau aux Fruits à l'Ancienne (Old-Fashioned Fruit Cake)

Ingredients

- 2 cups mixed dried fruits (raisins, currants, cherries)
- 1/2 cup rum or orange juice
- 1 cup flour
- 1/2 cup butter, softened
- 1/2 cup brown sugar
- 2 eggs
- 1/2 tsp cinnamon
- 1/4 tsp nutmeg

Instructions

1. Soak dried fruits in rum overnight.
2. Preheat oven to 325°F (165°C). Grease a loaf pan.
3. Cream butter and sugar, then beat in eggs.
4. Mix in flour, cinnamon, and nutmeg. Fold in soaked fruits.
5. Bake for 1 hour.

Oeufs en Gelée (Eggs in Aspic)

Ingredients

- 4 hard-boiled eggs, halved
- 2 cups chicken broth
- 1 tbsp gelatin
- 1/4 cup diced ham
- 1 tbsp parsley, chopped

Instructions

1. Dissolve gelatin in warm chicken broth.
2. Pour a thin layer into molds and chill until set.
3. Place eggs, ham, and parsley in molds. Pour in the remaining broth.
4. Chill for 3 hours before serving.

Pain d'Épices Québécois (Quebec Gingerbread)

Ingredients

- 2 cups flour
- 1/2 cup molasses
- 1/2 cup brown sugar
- 1/2 cup butter, melted
- 1 tsp cinnamon
- 1/2 tsp ginger
- 1/2 tsp baking soda
- 1/2 cup milk

Instructions

1. Preheat oven to 350°F (175°C). Grease a loaf pan.
2. In a bowl, mix flour, cinnamon, ginger, and baking soda.
3. In another bowl, mix molasses, brown sugar, butter, and milk.
4. Combine wet and dry ingredients. Pour into pan.
5. Bake for 45-50 minutes.

www.ingramcontent.com/pod-product-compliance
Lightning Source LLC
LaVergne TN
LVHW081342060526
838201LV00055B/2807